HEAVEN OR HELL

A Future Residence Guide

by Kirk Hille

CONCORDIA PUBLISHING HOUSE • SAINT LOUIS

Copyright © 2006 Concordia Publishing House
3558 S. Jefferson Ave., St. Louis, MO 63118-3968
1-800-325-3040 • www.cph.org

All rights reserved. Unless specifically noted, no part of this publication may be reproduced, stored in a retrieval system, or transmitted, in any form or by any means, electronic, mechanical, photocopying, recording, or otherwise, without the prior written permission of Concordia Publishing House.

The purchaser of this publication is allowed to reproduce the marked portions contained herein for use with this curriculum. These resources may not be transferred or copied to another user.

Written by Kirk Hille
Edited by Mark Sengele

Scripture quotations are taken from the HOLY BIBLE, NEW INTERNATIONAL VERSION®. NIV®. Copyright © 1973, 1978, 1984 by International Bible Society. Used by permission of Zondervan Publishing House. All rights reserved.

Quotation marked AE is from Luther's Works, American Edition: volume 21 copyright © 1956 by Concordia Publishing House, all rights reserved.

This publication may be available in braille, in large print, or on cassette tape for the visually impaired. Please allow 8 to 12 weeks for delivery. Write to the Library for the Blind, 7550 Watson Rd., St. Louis, MO 63119-4409; call toll-free 1-888-215-2455; or visit the Web site: www.blindmission.org.

Manufactured in the United States of America
Your comments and suggestions concerning the material are appreciated. Please write the Editor of Youth Materials, Concordia Publishing House, 3558 S. Jefferson Ave., St. Louis, MO 63118-3968.

1 2 3 4 5 6 7 8 9 10   15 14 13 12 11 10 09 08 07 06

Table of Contents

INTRODUCTION	8
1. So, You Are Thinking of Relocating	12
2. What Are Your Options? A Tour of Heaven and Hell	22
3. How Did They Come to Be? A History of Heaven and Hell	30
4. Who Lives There? A Population Profile of Heaven and Hell	40
5. What Is There to Do? Employment in Heaven and Hell	48
6. Preparing for Your Move	56

INTRODUCTION

Why This Study?

The study is designed to focus on the truth of Jesus Christ, our Lord and Savior. Through the study of God's Word, the participants will gain a greater understanding of what Scripture really teaches about heaven and hell. More important, this study seeks to help the faithful remain focused on the truths found within God's Word.

Locations

To enhance interest in this study, consider taking students on field trips or holding sessions in unusual locations. If transportation is available and time constraints allow, arrange to meet for each numbered session in or around the following:

1. A graveyard or mortuary
2. A garden, jail cell, or both
3. A monument or museum
4. A busy restaurant or other gathering place
5. A shopping, recreation, or employment center
6. A moving equipment rental agency or warehouse

If you are limited in how far you can go, consider places on your property that could be substituted:

1. Anywhere departed souls are remembered
2. A garden spot, furnace room, or both
3. A library or old photo display
4. A nearby home
5. A playground or workroom
6. A storeroom or safely parked truck

Preparing to Teach

As you prepare to teach this challenging study, you will need to allow adequate preparation time. As the leader, you should read all the text for each session in advance of class time. You may want to assign participants to read the text as a way of preparing for class time. For each class session make copies of the Student Leaflet in sufficient quantity for the class participants. Student Leaflets should be distributed at the time indicated in the leader directions.

Each of the six studies in this book follows a similar format: the lesson focus and a simple outline of the study are provided at the beginning of each lesson. The introductory statements are followed by detailed leader's directions and reproducible Student Leaflets. The leader's materials include a series of commentaries on the Bible text. The leader should summarize this material in order to present the information concerning the text to students. Following each lesson section are "Try This" activities. These active learning components are designed to help students better relate to the lesson. Each activity helps students to gain a stronger understanding of the text by connecting it to real-life experiences.

Basic class supplies should include pens or pencils for each student, blank paper, and a dry-erase board or equivalent (chalkboard, newsprint pad and easel) with appropriate markers or chalk. Encourage participants to bring along their own Bibles. Keep a supply of Bibles on hand for visitors or students who do not bring their own. The lesson outline suggests supplies needed for each section of the lesson.

Each study is completely outlined for the leader, including suggested lengths of time recommended for each portion of the study. The suggested times total approximately sixty minutes. In some cases, depending on class participation, it may be necessary to use additional time or omit portions of the lesson.

Leader's directions also contain instructions for when to have students work together as a whole group or when to break out into smaller groups of two to four students. These breakout directions are designed to facilitate more intimate discussions of the material. If your numbers are small, you may choose to ignore these breakout suggestions. In some cases, you may wish to have the whole group discuss the topic together instead of breaking into smaller groups.

Most of us perform better when there are no "surprises." As leader, you are encouraged to review each lesson fully, well in advance of its presentation. Materials can then be tailored to your individual students' preferences as well as your own.

Adapting These Studies

In some cases, it may be desirable to split lessons and use them over more than one session. Such adaptations are appropriate, perhaps even necessary, for the best possible results. You may wish to adapt one or more lessons for a youth night, retreat, or lock-in format. It may be necessary to supply additional questions or discussion starters for use by your group in these situations.

Adults and youth—even parents and their teenagers—can study these lessons together. While such classes are rare in most churches, there are certain benefits to discussing matters of faith in intergenerational groups. This is especially true when addressing difficult sections of Scripture.

It is necessary to be sensitive to the needs of both youth and adults when leading intergenerational groups.

Provide leadership opportunities for young people and adults. Let adults and youth share reading responsibilities, breakout-group leadership tasks, and response reporting duties.

Facilitate interaction. Unless they have had opportunity to study together before, some youth and adults may be initially reluctant to share answers with one another. Use opening group questions and sharing time to level the playing field for youth and adults.

Set a comfort level. Help groups to understand that not everyone will want to share, read aloud for the group, or answer every question. Help groups work toward a level of trust with one another.

Introduction

So, You Are THINKING of Relocating

Only a few years will pass before I go on the journey of no return. (Job 16:22)

LESSON 1

Lesson Objective

Through this lesson, students will become interested in this study of heaven and hell and discover misconceptions regarding mortality.

Lesson Outline

Activity	Suggested Time	Materials Needed
Introduction and Invitation **Try This:** *CONFIDENTIAL CONSIDERATIONS*	10 minutes	None Copies of Student Leaflet 1, scissors, envelopes
Two Certainties in Life: Death and Judgment **Try This:** *OBITUARY OVERVIEW*	20 minutes	Copies of Student Leaflet 1, newsprint or whiteboard Newspaper obituaries
Two Destinations in Death: Heaven and Hell **Try This:** *MAKING A MOVE*	20 minutes	None Copies of Student Leaflet 1
Conclusion and Challenge	5 minutes	None

Introduction and Invitation (10 minutes)

Cartoons and jokes abound regarding heaven and hell. Consider capturing student attention and introducing the theme of each session with a humorous illustration. One source for images might be *The Far Side*, a widely syndicated cartoon produced by Gary Larson from 1980–1994. This comic often depicted speculations regarding death, heaven, and hell using humorous images. The following joke might also be used to begin this session:

> A famous professor, an exchange student, and an elderly pastor happened to be sharing a private airplane on a sightseeing tour of the Middle East. High above the rocky desert, far from any landing strip, the plane's engine suddenly burst into flame and sputtered to a stop. The pilot, clearly distressed, announced, "My friends, I am sorry, but the plane is going to crash, and we only have three parachutes. Since I have a family, I hope you will forgive me for using one of them." He quickly strapped on the parachute, opened the door, and bailed out of the airplane. The professor, who had been sitting next to the pilot, turned and said, "I'm afraid I will have to take one of the remaining parachutes since I am one of the smartest men on earth and my death would be a great loss to humanity." With that, he followed the pilot out the door. The pastor turned to the young student and said, "My daughter, I have had a good life and am certain of eternity. Please, take the remaining parachute and enjoy God's deliverance." The student smiled and responded, "We can both enjoy God's deliverance, pastor. One of the smartest men on

earth just jumped out of the plane wearing my backpack!"

Say an opening prayer, such as the following:

> Heavenly Father, thank You for the gift of this life and the certainty of eternity when it is done. Send Your Holy Spirit to guide our discussion and study of what You have revealed to us concerning death and what follows. In the name of Jesus, our great deliverer. Amen.

> **TRY THIS: CONFIDENTIAL CONSIDERATIONS**
>
> Hand out copies of Student Leaflet 1, scissors, and an envelope for each student. Have students cut off the Confidential Considerations section of the Student Leaflet. Then have the students circle "yes," "no," or "maybe" after each statement without showing their answers to anyone else! When they are finished, have them seal their sheets in the envelopes and write their names on the outsides. Collect the envelopes and explain that they will have the opportunity to take the same inventory again and compare their answers to those they just put in the envelopes at the end of the study, in order to see if any of their answers have changed. This activity is primarily intended to pique the interest of the group, but if the students wish to discuss any of the items, skip ahead to the Confident Conclusions section in Session 6 on page 61.

Two Certainties in Life: Death and Judgment (20 minutes)

Ask a student volunteer to read the paragraph at the beginning of Student Leaflet 1, "So, You Are Thinking of Relocating." Ask students, **Whom do you know that has died? At what age did they die?** List the names and ages on newsprint or whiteboard for all to see. Then ask, **Is there any way to know for sure when you will die?** Students will likely say no. If they suggest suicide, point out that many who attempt suicide are surprised when they survive, while others who intend to live are surprised to die.

> Challenge the group to guess the top five causes of death for teens ages 15–19 in the United States. Compare their guesses with the following data from the Centers for Disease Control and Prevention (or visit the CDC Web site at www.cdc.gov for the most current statistics). Note that for the majority death comes as a surprise.
>
> 1. Accidents, especially automobile (48.5%)
> 2. Homicides (15.2%)
> 3. Suicides (11.7%)
> 4. Cancers (5.4%)
> 5. Heart Diseases (3.4%)

Ask your group, **What do you experience after you die?** List their responses on newsprint or whiteboard. If any responses are not biblically accurate, do not criticize the responses directly. Rather, invite the group to comment by saying, **Do you all agree that is what happens?** If students all agree with an unbiblical response, mark it with a star and note, **I'm going to mark that idea for us to** consider later, since I am not sure it agrees with what Scripture teaches about death. Remember to return to the idea when appropriate later in the study!

If the group does not raise the idea of judgment, ask, **Do Christians face judgment by God after they die, or is judgment only for unbelievers?** Pass around Bibles to any students who have not brought their own, and ask for volunteers to look up and read the following passages:

2 Corinthians 5:10 "For we must all appear before the judgment seat of Christ, that each one may receive what is due him for the things done while in the body, whether good or bad."

Hebrews 9:27–28 "Just as man is destined to die once, and after that to face judgment, so Christ was sacrificed once to take away the sins of many people; and He will appear a second time, not to bear sin, but to bring salvation to those who are waiting for Him."

Point out to the group that one aspect of death Scripture describes as certain is that we and all people will someday have our lives judged by God. Ask, **Since Christ takes away the sins of those who trust in Him, how is the judgment of believers different from unbelievers?** (We do not receive the punishment due us for the bad we have done, since Christ has taken it for us.) Ask for another volunteer to look up and read aloud the following passage, and discuss, **Do those who trust in Christ need to be afraid of God's judgment?** (No—we trust in God's perfect love, made available to us through Jesus' death and resurrection.)

> If anyone acknowledges that Jesus is the Son of God, God lives in him and he in God. And so we know and rely on the love God has for us. God is love. Whoever lives in love lives in God, and God in him. In this way, love is made complete among us so that we will have confidence on the day of judgment, because in this world we are like Him. There is no fear in love. But perfect love drives out fear, because fear has to do with punishment. The one who fears is not made perfect in love. (1 John 4:15–18)

TRY THIS: *OBITUARY OVERVIEW*

Cut out obituary notices from a local paper, and hand one out to every student. If you have a large group, you may need to make photocopies to ensure that you have enough. Invite the students to calculate the age of the person at death and to discuss what the notices say—and don't say—about the person. Ask,

Do they give the cause of death? (Usually, though in very general terms)

Do they describe the person's occupation? (Often they tell where someone worked.)

Do they say who the person's next of kin are? (Almost always)

Is there any evidence for whether the person described had faith in Christ or not? (The obituary may talk about church membership, but it is not likely to talk about the individual's faith life.)

> **Do any of the notices say anything bad about the person? Why not?** (It is quite unlikely that any will. Our culture is extremely reluctant to publicly pass judgment on the dead, since to do so would be to acknowledge that we ourselves face judgment.)
>
> **Do newspaper obituaries more resemble the judgment of God on believers or on unbelievers?** (Believers, since there is recognition of relationships, achievements, and positive qualities but no mention of wrongdoing)

Two Destinations in Death: Heaven and Hell (20 minutes)

Point out to students that in the same way that many people accept death but don't like to think about judgment, our culture is full of people who say they believe in heaven but deny the existence of hell! Yet Jesus Himself is among the many witnesses in Scripture who consistently affirm the existence of both destinations.

Encourage all the students to open up their Bibles to Luke 16:19–31. Ask three volunteers to read aloud and act out the parts of Jesus (who tells the parable), the rich man, and Abraham. After sharing the Bible text, discuss, **How does Jesus describe heaven?** (A place of comfort and reward where we are in the company of others, including such famous believers as Abraham) **How does Jesus describe hell?** (A place of torment, burning agony, and desire, separated from others) **What indicated that the rich man and Lazarus were both permanent residents of their new places?** (The chasm between heaven and hell prevented anyone from crossing from one to the other.) **What did the rich man want for his brothers?** (He wanted a special message or resurrection appearance that would convince them to repent and believe in their need for salvation.)

Explain to the group that while there are hundreds of references to heaven in the Bible, there are also dozens of references to hell. The Christian faith is both that those who trust in the salvation won by Christ's death and resurrection will ultimately join Him in heaven and also that those who reject His salvation will be separated from God in hell for eternity. These two are the only final destinations. Upcoming sessions in this study will examine them both in greater depth.

> **TRY THIS:** *MAKING A MOVE*
>
> Direct student attention to the Student Leaflet section titled How to Make Your Move. Encourage the students to think of an ideal community, a place they would rather live if they had the choice. Using the questions, ask them to compare their ideal community to where they currently live and consider what moving there might involve. Allow students to work together and share their answers with a partner. Then invite volunteers to discuss their answers with the group until everyone has had the opportunity to share. Then discuss:
>
> **Could these same considerations be applied to our future move through death into eternity? How does someone learn more about moving to heaven or hell?** (God reveals what we can know about them through His Word, the Bible.)

How can we prepare in advance a place in either heaven or hell? (Only through faith in Christ and His work for us are we prepared for heaven. On our own we merely reject that gift.)

Is it possible to take anything with you? (Scripture says we "store up . . . treasures in heaven" through service to God, though we do not know what form that treasure might take. See Matthew 6:20.)

How can you be sure you are united with family and friends for eternity? (Only the communion of saints, the fellowship of those who trust in Christ and join Him in heaven, can provide an eternal unity. While we *cannot* guarantee another person's inclusion, we *can* share our faith in Christ with them.)

Conclusion and Challenge (5 minutes)

Announce that the next session will include a tour of heaven and hell. Encourage students to bring photos, songs, written descriptions, and video or DVD clips (if you have the equipment to show them) in order to compare popular ideas of what heaven and hell are like with what Scripture reveals about them.

Close with a prayer,

> Loving God, thank You for sending Christ Jesus to take our punishment so that we need not fear Your judgment but can look forward through faith to eternity in heaven with You after we leave this life. Guide our study in the coming sessions so that we can better understand and share with others Your message of repentance and salvation. In Jesus' name. Amen.

So, You Are Thinking of RELOCATING

Get Ready!

Once you have made arrangements and confirmed reservations in your new community, you will need to prepare for the move itself by discarding or packing your possessions and bringing closure to relationships or ensuring that they continue through future contacts. Answer and discuss the following:

What are three possessions you would most want to take with you in a move?

Who are three people you would most want to take with you or keep in contact with?

Confidential Considerations

After each statement, circle "yes," "no," or "maybe," but don't show your answers to anyone else! Put your thoughts in an envelope, seal it up, and write your name on the outside.

1. Only old people really need to think about death.
   Yes   No   Maybe
2. Children who die are considered innocent before God.
   Yes   No   Maybe
3. A few people, like Hitler, are bad, but most are basically good.
   Yes   No   Maybe
4. God sends good people to heaven and only really bad people to hell.
   Yes   No   Maybe
5. God created hell as a place to punish people who make Him angry.
   Yes   No   Maybe
6. Heaven is a quiet, airy place where spirits float around on clouds.
   Yes   No   Maybe
7. Hell is an interesting place where you can party with famous people.
   Yes   No   Maybe
8. Heaven is whatever you want it to be, which is different for everyone.
   Yes   No   Maybe
9. After you die, your spirit comes back as a different person or animal.
   Yes   No   Maybe
10. When small children or really good people die they become angels.
    Yes   No   Maybe
11. Spirits of those who die tragically can hang around and haunt places.
    Yes   No   Maybe
12. There are no guarantees regarding where you go when you die.
    Yes   No   Maybe

Student Leaflet 1
Heaven or Hell: A Future Residence Guide © 2006
Concordia Publishing House. Okay to copy.

So, You Are Thinking of RELOCATING

Good for you! An old saying states that two things are certain in life: death and taxes! In fact, not everyone pays taxes, but all people, without exception, sooner or later leave life on earth. As a young person, you may be unprepared to make this move, thinking it unlikely to occur anytime soon. Yet tens of thousands of teens die every year in North America alone, and the vast majority of them are surprised by their sudden departure. Those who take the journey discover that death is not only a destruction of the body, but also a relocation of the spirit with one of two ultimate destinations: heaven or hell. This brochure is the first in a series designed to help you consider the move and your two relocation options: what they are like, who lives there, and how to prepare for your relocation to one or the other!

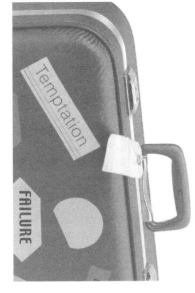

HOW TO MAKE YOUR MOVE

Do Research!

Before any move, it is best to research your possible future locations: What is the community like? What employment and recreational opportunities does it offer? What are the pros and cons of moving there? In the space below, brainstorm the pros and cons of living in your community, and compare them to what you think the pros and cons would be of your ideal community—someplace you might rather live!

MY COMMUNITY

Pros:

Cons:

MY IDEAL COMMUNITY

Pros:

Cons:

Make Reservations!

After deciding on a preferred future location, you will want to determine what it would take to relocate there. How many of the following questions can you answer about your ideal community?

If it is in another country, what does it take to get a passport and visa or to change citizenship?

How do you go about arranging housing and employment there before your move?

Will you need to exchange currency, get new identification, or learn new local laws?

Do you know anyone there who could help you?

Punishment	Eternal Life
HELL	HEAVEN
↓	↑

YOU ARE HERE

CROSSROADS

What Are Your Options?

A Tour of Heaven and Hell

Then they will go away to eternal punishment, but the righteous to eternal life. (Matthew 25:46)

LESSON
2

Lesson Objective

Through the study of the Scriptures, students will begin to understand and contrast the true characteristics of heaven and hell.

Lesson Outline

Activity	Suggested Time	Materials Needed
Introduction and Invitation **TRY THIS:** *BEST OR BUST*	15 minutes	None Newsprint or white board
Heaven: The Ultimate Paradise **TRY THIS:** *RIPPING RECOGNITION*	15 minutes	Copies of Student Leaflet 2, newsprint or whiteboard Magazines
Hell: The Ultimate Prison **TRY THIS:** *IMAGE INVESTIGATION*	20 minutes	Copies of Student Leaflet 2, newsprint or whiteboard Television, DVD and CD players
Conclusion and Challenge	5 minutes	

Introduction and Invitation (15 minutes)

Consider using the following joke or an appropriate cartoon to begin this session.

> A very wealthy man becomes a Christian and immediately gives the vast majority of his fortune to relief organizations and charities that serve the poor. He reconciles relationships with his family, friends, and former employees; joins a church; and spends all his time serving God to the best of his ability. As a result, when the time comes for him to die, God gives him the special privilege of taking one carry-on bag of valuables with him to heaven. When the man arrives in heaven, saints and angels all gather round to see what the man thought to bring, since no one had ever been allowed this special privilege. As the man proudly opens his bag to reveal row upon row of gleaming, solid gold bars, a wave of laughter sweeps through the crowd. "Pavement?" they roar. "He brought pavement!"

Open with prayer,

> Heavenly Father, Your glory is beyond compare, and what You have prepared for those who trust in Your Son is beyond human imagination. Through the power of Your Holy Spirit, open our hearts and minds to better understand and respond to what Your Word

reveals regarding our future destinations. Through Christ Jesus our Lord. Amen.

> **TRY THIS:** *BEST OR BUST*
>
> Before class, write the four questions listed below on newsprint or whiteboard. The point of this session is to contrast heaven and hell. Ask each student to share the best and the worst vacations he or she ever took by answering the four questions posted for today:
>
> Where did you go?
>
> What did you see?
>
> What did you do?
>
> Who were you with?
>
> If you have more than five students, consider forming smaller groups of three to five members each. Give each person one minute to share his or her experience. Once everyone has had a chance to speak, vote on the best of the best and the worst of the worst vacations. Consider giving small prizes to those with the overall best and worst stories.

Move into the next part of the study by explaining, **As good and bad as your experiences were, they cannot compare to what the Bible reveals about the wonders of heaven and the horrors of hell.**

Heaven: The Ultimate Paradise (15 minutes)

Before class, draw a vertical line to divide a sheet of newsprint or a whiteboard into two columns. At the top, label the left side "Heaven" and the right side "Hell." Write the following words down the right edge to create five categories: "See," "Hear," "Smell," "Taste," "Touch."

Hand out copies of Student Leaflet 2. Ask a student to begin reading aloud the section entitled Heaven: The Ultimate Paradise. At the end of the first paragraph, invite another student to continue reading and then another, until it is complete.

Ask the students to consider the description of heaven just read. Ask, **What would you expect to see on a tour of heaven?** Write their responses on the board. Then ask, **What would you hear?** Continue until each category is discussed. Possible answers include the following:

See (God, angels, saints, gold, jewels, city, mountains, trees)

Hear (Music, praise, prayers, shouts of joy)

Smell (Incense)

Taste (A feast, fresh fruit, crystal water)

Touch (Gold, fine linen, crystal water, healing leaves)

Have students turn to a partner and ask each other the following questions, giving them a minute for each question. Answers for each will vary.

What, if anything, in the description of heaven surprises you? (Answers will vary but should reflect the information shared earlier.)

What about heaven might surprise your friends? (Probably quite a few things)

What part of the description do you like best? (Answers will vary. Encourage all students to share their answers to this question.)

Then have each pair pick one of the Scripture references from this section of the Student Leaflet to look up and read to the class.

> **Try This: Ripping Recognition**
>
> Keep the pairs formed above if they are still working well together, or ask the students to quickly find a new partner. Give each pair a news or travel magazine and no more than five minutes to find and rip out a photo that they both agree best represents some aspect of heaven as described in Scripture. Have one person from each pair show the picture to the class while the other explains why they chose it. Then give the pairs no more than three minutes to rip out a second picture they think might represent some aspect of hell. Have each pair again share their picture and reasoning with the class, in preparation for the next section of the lesson.

Hell: The Ultimate Prison (20 minutes)

Ask a student volunteer to begin reading aloud the second section of the Student Leaflet under the heading Hell: The Ultimate Prison. At the end of each paragraph, invite another student to continue the reading until it is complete. Ask students to consider the description just read. What would they expect to see on a tour of hell? Write their responses on the newsprint or whiteboard. Then ask, **What would you hear?** Continue until each category is discussed. Possible answers might include these:

See (Nothing, no one, darkness, flames)

Hear (Weeping, or nothing)

Smell (Sulfur, smoke, burning flesh)

Taste (Smoke, broken teeth)

Feel (Fire, agony)

Have students turn to a new partner and ask each other the following three questions, giving them a minute for each question. Have each pair pick a Scripture reference to look up and share with the class.

What, if anything, in the description of hell surprises you? (Answers will vary.)

What about hell might surprise your friends? (Answers will vary.)

Why do you think more people claim to believe in heaven than believe in hell? (Answers will vary. In general, more people like to think of God as loving; they don't want to deal with the image of a God who condemns unrepentant sinners.)

> **Try This: Image Investigation**
>
> If students have brought DVDs, photos, or songs depicting heaven or hell, take some time to examine and discuss the images they present of heaven and hell. In case the students have not brought any, you may wish to have some materials prepared for discussion, or simply ask the students about books, movies, songs, and ads they have experienced. Discuss with students which images most accurately reflect what Scripture reveals?

Conclusion and Challenge (5 minutes)

Announce that the next session will discuss what Scripture reveals about how and why heaven and hell came to exist. Challenge students to ask at least five people this week whether they think heaven and hell exist and, if so, what they are like. Ask students to be prepared to share the answers next week. Encourage them to invite the people they ask to join the class!

Close with prayer:

> Holy God, thank You for giving us the assurance of an eternity spent with You in paradise when we deserve only punishment in hell. Forgive us for times we have taken Your gifts for granted, and strengthen our faith that we may be able to share Your promise of heaven with others as we talk with them about our eternal destination. In Jesus' name. Amen.

A Tour of HEAVEN and HELL

pure, powerful, and stunning city built of gold and jewels, with views, variety, and wealth beyond comparison with anything on earth. The light of God's glory will shine like the sun without ceasing, the wealth and honor of human kings will be commonplace, and there will be complete safety **(Revelation 21:6-26)**. Eternal life will be supplied by the Holy Spirit as a crystal river running through the center of the great street of the city, feeding a tree of life with continual crops of fresh fruit and healing for all people. There paradise will be restored to God's faithful, who will rule FOREVER as His royal family **(Revelation 22:1-5)**.

Hell: THE ULTIMATE PRISON

Best known for its UNQUENCHABLE FIRE and **unimaginable torment**, hell is the ultimate destination for demons and human spirits who reject God and His salvation. Sometimes referred to as **"THE ABYSS,"** a term meaning "a deep, dark pit," hell is even less well known than heaven; although, it is popular among some to suggest it as a destination for others. Frequent mention of raging fires in hell not-ment of God on those who reject Him **(Matthew 3:12; 5:21-22; Luke 16:23-24; Hebrew 10:26-27; James 3:6)**. Smoke and burning sulfur are among its torments **(Revelation 9:2; 14:9-11)**, and the eternal destruction of unbelievers, death, and Hades, the *place of the dead*, is described as a lake of burning sulfur **(Revelation 20:13-15; 21:8)**. However, depictions of hell's torments also include being devoured by worms that do not die **(Isaiah 66:24; Mark 9:43-49)**.

Commonly mentioned in descriptions of hell is blackest darkness, desolation, and silence **(1 Samuel 2:9-10; 2 Peter 2:17; Jude 13)**, where the wicked weep and gnash their teeth **(Matthew 8:12; 22:13; 25:30)**. In contrast to heaven, hell is a place of everlasting destruction and separation from the presence and majesty of God **(2 Thessalonians 1:9)**, and there is never any rest from torment **(Revelation 14:11)**. Originally established as a gloomy dungeon where disobedient angels are bound with everlasting chains to await Judgment Day **(2 Peter 2:4; Jude 6)**, hell has become a prison also for the spirits of disobedient humans **(1 Peter 3:19-20)**. Confinement may be completely solitary, since no mention is ever made of individuals encountering each other in hell.

Even demons dread going to hell **(Luke 8:31)**. Therefore, Jesus, the only human to visit and return, stated that it would be better, if you had to make a choice, to gouge out your eye or cut off your hand than to go there **(Matthew 5:29-30; 18:8-9)**.

HEAVEN:

The Ultimate Paradise

Best known as the dwelling place of God (**Deuteronomy 26:15**) and for its extensive exports of everything good (**Malachi 3:10**), **heaven is the ultimate destination** for anyone who trusts in God's salvation through Jesus. Heaven is the *private residence* of God and His servants, so no tourism is allowed. However, Jesus was able to describe heaven from personal experience (**John 3:12–13**), and occasionally God's people on official business have been given glimpses of heaven, or, in the case of John the apostle, a virtual tour.

Job described it as "AWESOME" and orderly, full of God's servants and light (**Job 25:2–3**). David and other psalm writers described it as filled with the **greatness, power, glory, majesty, splendor, wealth, and honor** of **God** (**1 Chronicles 29:11–12**); a place where God laughs at the vanity of earthly kings (**Psalm 2:4**); and the place from which He considers everything done on earth (**Psalm 33:13–15**). Among the prophets given glimpses into heaven, Micaiah saw God on His throne surrounded by His servants (**1 Kings 22:19**), and Isaiah described the mighty, mysterious angels known as seraphs that surround the throne and rock the house with their "smoking" songs of worship (**Isaiah 6:1–4**).

Jesus depicted heaven as the future site of a great feast for all God's people from all over the earth (**Matthew 8:11**), where the guardian angels always see the face of God (**Matthew 18:10**), where justice and comfort are given to the faithful who suffered on earth (**Luke 16:25**), and where He would prepare rooms for all who would follow Him (**John 14:1–4**). The author of Hebrews describes heaven as *a place of rest*, where it is always a holiday (**Hebrews 4:9–10**), as a place where God's promises and glory far exceed anything on earth (**Hebrews 8:5–6**), and as **a mountain city** where God lives with **joyful angels** and perfected humans (**Hebrews 12:22–24**). Peter notes that it is where we inherit the wonders Christ won for us (**1 Peter 1:3–5**).

John, given the most extensive revelation, describes the **astounding beauty, POWER,** and WEALTH OF GOD ON HIS THRONE, surrounded by the **thunder of**

> All heaven awaits Judgment Day, when God's righteousness and *victory over evil* will BE REVEALED to all people

His justice, the light of His Spirit, and the peace of a calm crystal lake, all at the same time. There God is worshiped by all-seeing seraphs, fantastic angels that resemble the most powerful, humble, intelligent, and noble of all God's creatures. Also surrounding the throne are the greatest of God's human servants, dressed in fine linen and wearing crowns, bowing down in worship and gratitude (**Revelation 4:1–5:8**). Christ, all-powerful and all-seeing, sits on the throne and enjoys loud musical praise, incense, and prayers from people of all nations, millions of angels, and all creation (**Revelation 5:6–14**).

All heaven awaits Judgment Day, when God's righteousness and victory over evil will be revealed to all people (**Revelation 15:1–4**). Then a new heaven and earth where God will live with us will be unveiled, and there will be no more tears, death, mourning, crying, or pain (**Revelation 21:1–5**). The Holy Spirit and eternal life will be freely given to all those who have become God's children in a beautiful, brilliant city built by God on a great mountain for His people from every age.

How Did They Come to Be?

A History of Heaven and Hell

Come, you who are blessed by My Father; take your inheritance, the kingdom prepared for you since the creation of the world. (Matthew 25:34)

LESSON

3

Lesson Objective

Through their study of God's Word, students will consider the nature and necessity of heaven and hell.

Lesson Outline

Activity	Suggested Time	Materials Needed
Introduction and Invitation **Try This:** Language Limits	15 minutes	None Prepared index cards
Heaven: A Master-Planned Community **Try This:** Time Trials	20 minutes	Copies of Student Leaflet 3 String and small heavy object
Hell: A Demonic Detention Center **Try This:** Garbage or Glory	15 minutes	Copies of Student Leaflet 3 Trash/garbage, garbage bags, trash can, recycling container, signs, gloves
Conclusion and Challenge	5 minutes	

Introduction and Invitation (15 minutes)

As your group gathers, ask, **Who asked five people whether heaven and hell exist this past week? What did they say? What did they think heaven and hell were like?** Allow time for discussion.

The following joke or an appropriate cartoon might also be used to begin this session:

> A young boy was grieving over the death of his beloved dog, and his parents were trying to comfort him by assuring him that his pet was in "dog heaven." Having just begun to learn about heaven and hell at church, the boy had many questions. He asked, "What do dogs do in heaven?"
>
> His parents answered, "I suppose they get to eat whatever they want and run around all day chasing squirrels."
>
> The boy thought for a moment, then asked, "So is dog heaven the same place as squirrel hell?"

Open in prayer.

> Heavenly Father, we sometimes struggle to comprehend the realities of heaven and hell. Guide our study through Your Holy Spirit,

who helps us to understand Your Word and to have faith even beyond our understanding. In Christ Jesus. Amen.

> **TRY THIS:** *LANGUAGE LIMITS*
>
> Before class, write each of the following words on an index card or scrap of paper: *firefly, sunrise, shooting star, cliffhanger, heartbreak, skyscraper*. Play a game of charades by asking six different volunteers to each take a turn acting out one of the words for the rest of the group to guess. Watch to see whether the actors portray the literal meaning of the words' parts (i.e., pretending to be burned to indicate fire and flapping arms to indicate fly) or the figurative meaning of the words as a whole (i.e., pretending to fly around and flash light to indicate firefly), so that you can explain the difference between literal and figurative meanings, if necessary.
>
> When all the words have been guessed ask, **What do these six words have in common?** The game of charades will likely help the students to guess the answer—all six words are metaphors, words that figuratively and poetically describe the appearance of something but are not literally what they describe. To explain, ask the students to guess the metaphor we use to describe each of the actual meanings below:
>
> - light of our nearest star appearing above the horizon as a result of earth's diurnal rotation (sunrise)
> - a winged nocturnal beetle that produces intermittent light by oxidation of luciferin (firefly)
> - a meteor striking the earth's atmosphere, thus appearing as a temporary streak of light in the night sky (shooting star)
> - a suspenseful contest or adventure (cliffhanger)
> - a feeling of intense grief (heartbreak)
> - a very tall building (skyscraper)
>
> Note that the sun does not actually rise, fireflies are neither on fire nor flies, shooting stars are neither shot nor stars, cliffhangers may have nothing to do with hanging from a cliff, heartbreak does not mean anything is wrong with your cardiac muscle, and skyscrapers do not actually scrape anything off the sky. But each word is an easy and memorable way for us to describe a much more complicated subject. In the same way, the words we translate into English as "heaven" and "hell" are actually metaphors for places that are real but beyond our experience and difficult to describe. They are not part of our existence on earth, but we must use earthly images to understand them.

Heaven: A Master-Planned Community (20 minutes)

Hand out copies of Student Leaflet 3, and ask a student volunteer to begin reading aloud the Heaven: A Master-Planned Community section. At the end of the first paragraph, invite another student to continue the reading, then another, until it is complete.

Discuss the following with your group.

What, if anything, surprised you about the description of heaven's history? (Answers will vary. Some students may mention the rebellion of the angels as a surprising event.)

Why was heaven created? (Heaven serves as the dwelling place of God.)

Why is it natural to speak of heaven as "up" and "in the sky"? (The Greek and Hebrew words for "heaven" are the same words used for "sky" or "atmosphere.")

Do you think the speculations of physicists and science fiction writers that there might be parallel universes in dimensions we do not experience can be helpful to Christians trying to imagine where heaven might be, or would it be more helpful to not think about it? (While certainly speculative, this concept may be helpful to Christians struggling to understand the reality of a spiritual dimension that lies beyond our human experience.)

One of the first Russian cosmonauts to experience outer space is reported to have said, "I did not see God." How would you have answered him? (Despite his inability to see God, who exists as spirit, God is still just as real.)

> ### TRY THIS: *TIME TRIALS*
>
> Show students a piece of string no longer than your arm, and ask your group if they can make the string, or a least part of it, disappear. Tell them that they are not allowed to hide or destroy the string, but must make it invisible. Let students attempt this feat; congratulate any that succeed. If students are unwilling or unable to accomplish this task, take a small heavy object (a metal washer, toy figure, or eraser) and tie it securely to one end of the string. Hold the string on the opposite end from the object and begin spinning the object in a vertical circle, faster and faster, until the string is moving fast enough to become invisible to the human eye. (Be careful to aim the spinning object away from any students, in case it should come untied and fly off!)
>
> Ask students, **Why did the string become invisible?** (Our eyes are not designed to perceive such fast motion.) **Did the string cease to exist just because we could not see it? How do you know?** (No! Other evidence, such as the air disturbance and the fact that the string became visible again as it slowed indicates its continued existence.)
>
> **For us to experience something, it is not enough to be nearby in space; we must also share the same time frame. We don't experience things that happen before or after we are in this room, nor are we aware of things in the room right now that are too fast or outside the visible spectrum, such as subatomic particles or radio waves. In a similar way, heaven may be invisible to us now simply because it lies outside our time frame.**
>
> Ask volunteers to look up and read aloud the following verses:

Ecclesiastes 3:11 "He has made everything beautiful in its time. He has also set eternity in the hearts of men; yet they cannot fathom what God has done from beginning to end."

Romans 1:20 "For since the creation of the world God's invisible qualities—His eternal power and divine nature—have been clearly seen, being understood from what has been made, so that men are without excuse."

2 Corinthians 4:18 "So we fix our eyes not on what is seen, but on what is unseen. For what is seen is temporary, but what is unseen is eternal."

1 Timothy 1:17 "Now to the King eternal, immortal, invisible, the only God, be honor and glory for ever and ever. Amen."

2 Peter 3:8 "But do not forget this one thing, dear friends: With the Lord a day is like a thousand years, and a thousand years are like a day."

Discuss these questions with your whole group:

Is God confined to the same time frame as we are? (No)

Is there a connection between God's invisibility and an eternal time frame? (Evidence would indicate that there must be some connection.)

How then can we experience God? (We experience God directly where He confines Himself to our world as promised, in the person of Jesus, in His Word, and in the means of grace. We can experience Him indirectly, as Paul's Letter to the Romans notes, by observing His work in the world. We will experience Him ultimately when we join Him in His time frame: eternity!)

Hell: A Demonic Detention Center (15 minutes)

Direct attention to the section of the Student Leaflet entitled Hell: A Demonic Detention Center. Ask volunteers to read through this section, one paragraph at a time. Discuss the following as a group:

What, if anything, surprised you about the description of hell's history?

Why was hell created?

Why is it natural to speak of hell as "down" and "under the earth"?

> **TRY THIS: *GARBAGE OR GLORY***
>
> Bring out a bag or two of trash from your home, making sure it has a mixture of potentially recyclable items and nothing too gross in it. Better yet, if your time frame and setting allow it, send pairs from your group out into the neighborhood equipped with gloves and a bag to collect their own trash. Give students a time limit and offer a prize to the team that brings back the biggest bag! Have a volunteer wearing gloves open each bag and sort the items into two containers: a trash can labeled "garbage," and a recycling bin labeled "glory." After, or as the trash is sorted, discuss the following:

They say that one person's trash is another person's treasure, but is that always true? (No—some trash items are beyond redemption.)

What happens to our garbage: is it burned, or buried, or what? (Answers will vary. You may need to investigate the answer!)

Why is it essential that garbage and sewage be removed from our homes? (They would otherwise spread disease, draw pests, produce foul odors, clutter up our houses, and increase the risks of fire.)

How are garbage and recyclable items alike? (Both are considered trash in that they have outlived their usefulness.)

How are garbage and recyclable materials different? (Recycled items are remade into something new and live a new life.)

How is recycling like going to heaven and garbage disposal like going to hell? (Recycled items are remade and given a new life, just as those who trust in Christ will be redeemed, remade, and given a new life in heaven. Garbage items are discarded and burned or buried, just as those who reject Christ's redemption can neither remain nor be remade by God and so are destined for hell.)

What's wrong with putting garbage in the recycling box? (It pollutes the recyclable materials and can ruin the system.)

Why doesn't God allow those who reject Him and refuse to repent of their sins into heaven? (God does not take away our free will, nor will He allow human sin to pollute heaven and pervert His justice. Only through Christ's punishment and death in our place can the stain of human sin be removed, and only through His resurrection can we gain a new, eternal life.)

Conclusion and Challenge (5 minutes)

Announce that the next session will discuss the residents of heaven and hell. Challenge students to bring angel, saint, or demon pictures or paraphernalia they might encounter to the next session.

Close with a prayer,

> Holy God, thank You for redeeming us through the gift of Christ Jesus' life, death, and resurrection so that we can look forward to being remade and given a new life with You in heaven. Send Your Spirit, and work through us to share Your message of salvation with our friends and families, so that they need never be separated from You to suffer the torments of hell. In the name of our Savior, Jesus. Amen.

Hell: A Demonic Detention Center

In contrast to heaven, the place created for those who want to dwell with God, hell was created as an alternative for those who reject the true God. Originally, hell was created to be a detention center for demons, angels who rebelled against God, where they would be held for ultimate judgment (**Matthew 25:41; 1 Peter 3:18–20; 2 Peter 2:4**). However, after mankind fell into sin, those humans who went to their deaths in rebellion against God and without faith in His promised redemption had no alternative but to be housed in hell with the demons. There they begin their punishment even while awaiting the final judgment (**2 Peter 2:9**).

Hell experienced a population explosion when God used a flood to wipe the wicked off the face of the earth in the time of Noah (**1 Peter 3:19–20**) and a smaller population spike when God destroyed Sodom and Gomorrah (**Jude 6–7**). When Korah and his followers rebelled against God after Israel was rescued from slavery in Egypt, the ground opened up and swallowed them and all their possessions in judgment, separating them from God's fellowship forever and leading to the association of hell with an underground grave (**Numbers 16:30–33**).

This association was further strengthened by God's declaration that His wrath "burns to the realm of death below" (**Deuteronomy 32:22**) and use of the Hebrew word *Sheol* and the Greek word *Hades* to describe both the grave and the place of punishment for the wicked who rely on themselves, in contrast to the redeemed who trust in God (**Psalm 49:10–15; Proverbs 5:5**). However, the physical location of hell, like heaven, is a mystery not revealed by Scripture.

In the New Testament, the prison for the wicked, separated from God and awaiting final judgment is often referred to as "Gehenna," the name of a deep, narrow valley outside Jerusalem where the city's garbage was burned. In the Old Testament, Gehenna had been a place where wicked idolaters had burned their children alive as sacrifices to the false god Molech. So the word we translate "hell" had an association with the wicked who worship false gods and the destruction by fire of all that was unclean, worthless, and cast out of the city of God's presence. The metaphor perfectly matches the purpose of hell: judgment, punishment, destruction, and permanent separation from God for all those who choose evil and reject His redemption.

A History of Heaven and Hell

Heaven:

A MASTER-PLANNED COMMUNITY

Heaven is the ultimate Master-planned community, having been created by God, the Master Architect, to be His dwelling place and ours since the beginning of the world (Matthew 25:34).

The words we translate "heaven" also mean the sky, atmosphere, or visible universe in both the Hebrew and Greek—the languages in which the Bible was written. Earth's atmosphere is essential for our life, the place we encounter the sunlight and rain on which we depend, the lens through which we see the beauty of sunsets and the majesty of the universe, as well as the source of threatening winds and thunderstorms that test the quality of our works. No wonder it was named after the dwelling place of God!

The physical location of heaven is a mystery not revealed in Scripture and seems to be outside of, and perhaps parallel to, our physical universe (Job 23:3). From heaven, God is able to see everything that is done on earth, hear our prayers, provide for our needs, and intervene at any time **(Deuteronomy 26:15)**. In fact, angels are able to carry out God's will on earth while simultaneously seeing into heaven **(Matthew 18:10)**.

Important events in the history of heaven include the rebellion of many of God's angels, led by Satan, the accuser **(Job 1:6–12; 2:1–7)**. Although the devil was no match for God, our fall into sin allowed Satan to accuse humans in heaven until he was finally banished as a result of Christ's victory on the cross **(Luke 10:18; Revelation 12:3–11)**. Thus the coming of Christ to earth was a source of great rejoicing in heaven **(Luke 2:10–14)**, since it meant not only the casting down of Satan but eternal life in heaven for all those who trust in Christ **(Luke 15:7; John 6:33)**. When Christ returned to heaven, He was seated at God's right hand, where He is worshiped and continues to serve as Head of His Church **(Ephesians 1:20)**.

Currently, both the angels and the saints in heaven look forward to the Day of Judgment, when Christ will return to resurrect the dead, God will judge *will be Replaced with a new heaven and earth in harmony with each other (Matthew 24:35–36; 2 Peter 3:13; Revelation 21:1).* Until then, heaven is where the spirits of those who die with faith in Christ enjoy His presence and await His restoration of the world **(Acts 3:21; Ephesians 3:14–15; Revelation 6:9–11)**.

Who Lives There?

A Population Profile of Heaven and Hell

Whoever believes in Him is not condemned, but whoever does not believe stands condemned.

(John 3:18)

LESSON

4

Lesson Objective

Through the study of the Word, students will begin to understand the differences between angels, demons, saints, and lost souls.

Lesson Outline

Activity	Suggested Time	Materials Needed
Introduction and Invitation **TRY THIS:** *SAINT SIGHTINGS*	10 minutes	Angel, saint, or demon pictures Copies of Reproducible Page 4
Heaven: Home to Angels and the Saints **TRY THIS:** *EXCEPTIONAL EXAMPLES*	20 minutes	Copies of Student Leaflet 4 Paper, markers, colored pencils
Hell: Home to Demons and the Damned **TRY THIS:** *SCREWTAPE'S SUCCESSORS*	20 minutes	Copies of Student Leaflet 4 Paper and pens/pencils, *The Screwtape Letters*
Conclusion and Challenge	10 minutes	Hymnals and/or recording

Introduction and Invitation (10 minutes)

As your group gathers, examine any angel, saint, or demon pictures or paraphernalia students might have brought with them. Consider bringing your own images to share if you have any, or print some out from a quick Internet search of "angels," "saints," and "demons." The following joke or an appropriate cartoon might also be used to begin this session:

> Saint Peter and Satan were having an argument one day about baseball. Satan proposed a game to be played on neutral grounds between a select team from the heavenly host and his own handpicked boys. "Very well," said Peter. "But you realize, I hope, that we've got all the truly good players and the very best coaches." "I know, and that's all right," Satan answered. "We've got all the umpires."

Say an opening prayer,

> Heavenly Father, our world often fails to understand the nature of those who dwell with You in heaven and those who dwell apart from You in hell. Guide our study through Your Holy Spirit, so that we better understand what Your Word reveals about angels, saints, demons, and the damned. In Christ Jesus we pray. Amen.

TRY THIS: *SAINT SIGHTINGS*

To help remind your students how the lives of famous saints have affected the lives of even non-Christians, have the group divide into teams of two. Provide each team with a copy of Reproducible Page 4. Allow pairs a few minutes to think about their answers, and then challenge pairs to give the answers as you read each clue. Award points for each correct answer. Help students who may be struggling with answers by reminding them that in Spanish the word for "saint" is "*san*."

This saint spurs Texans to cheer: San Antonio.
This saint is an island of refuge for mariners: San Juan.
This saint is known for her angry eruptions: Saint Helen(s).
This saint is a sunny padre with a big naval base: San Diego.
This saint is famous for inspiring love notes: Saint Valentine.
This saint is a capital guy with a better-known twin: Saint Paul.
This saint gets the blame when California quakes: San Andreas.
This saint is famous for his bridge and cable cars: San Francisco.
This saint is known for his arch and cardinal virtues: Saint Louis.
This saint is credited with leaving gifts under trees: Saint Nicholas.
This saint has an Erie way of leading ships to the ocean: Saint Lawrence.
This saint is celebrated for bringing Good News to the Irish: Saint Patrick.

Heaven: Home to Angels and the Saints (20 minutes)

Hand out copies of Student Leaflet 4, and ask for a student volunteer to begin reading aloud the Heaven: Home to Angels and the Saints section. At the end of the first paragraph, invite another student to continue the reading until the section on the angels is complete. Ask,

Did anything surprise you about the description of angels? How is the Bible's description similar to or different from the ways you have seen angels portrayed in artwork, in movies, or even on Christmas cards? (The angels described in Scripture display masculine characteristics. They demonstrate power, and often their very presence strikes fear into the hearts of those who see them. Our contemporary media often presents angels as either whimsical pixies or beautiful women in flowing gowns with wings.)

Ask another volunteer to read aloud the section on the saints. Discuss,

Did anything surprise you about the description of saints? How is the Bible's definition similar to or different from the ways you have heard saints described in popular culture or even in church? (The world often defines saints in terms of their good behavior. Scripture shows us that the saints in heaven are in fact those saved and washed clean through the blood of Christ.)

TRY THIS: *EXCEPTIONAL EXAMPLES*

If your church contains artwork representing any saints, take your group on a short tour and discuss who and what the art represents. Many Christian churches recognize certain saints as exceptional examples of a faithful Christian life and death, naming congregations after them, depicting them in artwork, or even remembering them on a certain day. Some groups take this to an unhealthy extreme by attributing legends to these saints, encouraging prayer through them, and assigning them as patron saints for those with even the most remote connection. For example, Saint Ambrose is considered a patron saint of beekeepers because his preaching earned him the nickname "honey tongued," while Saint Isodore has been nominated as patron saint of the Internet because he published an early encyclopedia!

Scripture makes it clear that because Christ made us righteous before God, we can approach His throne directly without asking others to intercede for us (Hebrews 4:14–16). Yet we are also called to follow the example of other saints, and as saints to set an example for those who follow us. As Paul writes to Timothy, "Don't let anyone look down on you because you are young, but set an example for the believers in speech, in life, in love, in faith and in purity" (1 Timothy 4:12).

Distribute paper and markers or colored pencils to the group. Ask students to draw an icon, a symbol or picture of someone who has been an example of Christian faithfulness to them, or a reminder of someone to whom they would like to be an example of Christian faith. After ten minutes, have volunteers share what they created and why with the group.

Hell: Home to Demons and the Damned (20 minutes)

Direct students' attention to the section of the Student Leaflet titled Hell: Home to Demons and the Damned. Ask for volunteers to read this section, one paragraph at a time. Discuss as a group, **Did anything surprise you about the description of demons?** (Answers will vary.) **How is the Bible's description similar to or different from the ways you have seen demons portrayed in popular culture?** (Answers will vary.) **What one factor determines who will be among the damned?** (Their lack of trust in God's gift of salvation through Christ Jesus!)

TRY THIS: *SCREWTAPE'S SUCCESSORS*

In his popular book *The Screwtape Letters*, C. S. Lewis wrote a series of fictional letters from an experienced demon named Screwtape to his inexperienced nephew, Wormwood, on how to tempt and deceive a new Christian convert away from faith in Christ. If you have access to a copy of *The Screwtape Letters*, you might want to read letter II, III, or IV as an example.

Explain to your group that you would like them to work in pairs to write a short letter from the perspective of an experienced demon named Screwtape to a less experienced one named Wormwood. In their letter, they should explain the best ways to tempt a young person away from faith in Christ. Be sure to encourage your group to write more modern examples in their own words. Explain that groups will be asked to read their letters to the class. When the letters have been shared, ask, **Why are demons motivated to tempt humans away from faith?** (Probably out of hatred or bitterness) **How are they most successful?** (Answers will vary.) **Why might**

> **demons want to hide themselves and convince people that they don't exist?** (They are likely to be more successful at tempting and deceiving those who do not believe they exist.)

Conclusion and Challenge (10 minutes)

Encourage students to consider ways that angels and demons may be active influences in life as they know it and to write a more complete letter from Screwtape to be shared at the next session, which will look at the governments of heaven and hell. If you have a favorite recording of "A Mighty Fortress Is Our God" (*LW* 297/298; *AGPS* 50; *TLH* 262), you may want to close the session by playing it and reminding students that as powerful as demons may seem in this world, they are completely overwhelmed by God's Word and Spirit. If your group likes to sing, you might even lead them in singing this great anthem of faith.

Be sure to close in prayer.

> All-powerful God, thank You for the salvation and victory won for us by Christ Jesus over sin, death, and the devil. Protect us with Your mighty angels, and encourage us through Your Holy Spirit to remain strong in faith and to remember our calling to be Your saints, this week and forever. In Jesus' name we pray. Amen.

temptation (**1 Timothy 4:1–3**). Their leader is Satan, the accuser, also known as the devil, the destroyer, the dragon, the serpent, Beelzebub, the prince of demons, and the father of lies (**Luke 11:15; John 8:44; Revelation 9:11; 12:9**). Far from appearing as the horned, distorted figure in paintings and cartoons, demons may be quite attractive in appearance, since Satan masquerades as an angel of light (**2 Corinthians 11:14**), and those who belong to him are able to perform counterfeit miracles, signs, and wonders (**2 Thessalonians 2:9–10**). They prefer deception and distraction to direct confrontation (**1 Chronicles 21:1; Mark 4:15**). The number of demons is unknown, but it is thought that a third of the angels in heaven fell away and became demons at the time of Satan's rebellion (**Revelation 12:3–4**). Furthermore, a single person can be possessed by a legion of demons (**Mark 5:2–13**). Demons have been cast out of heaven and bound by the victory of Jesus on the cross so that they cannot accuse or overcome those who trust in Christ (**Luke 10:18–20; Revelation 12:7–12**). However, they are ferocious as they await their final judgment and banishment from the earth (**1 Peter 5:8; 2 Peter 2:4; Jude 6**).

The Damned

The damned are those humans who reject God and the salvation won for them by Christ Jesus (**Matthew 23:31–33; Mark 16:16; John 3:18; 2 Thessalonians 1:8–10; 2:12**). They may have been quite wealthy and successful on earth, well thought of, seemingly righteous, and even religious leaders (**Matthew 19:23; 23:15; Luke 16:22–23**). Yet, if they reject God and refuse to receive the salvation won through Christ, they will be condemned to hell (**John 3:18–20; 2 Thessalonians 2:12; Revelation 20:15**), where they will begin their punishment even while they await the final judgment (**2 Peter 2:4–9**). Therefore, many of those in hell are quite

25:41–46), in agony and full of regret for their rejection of God's message of salvation (**Luke 16:23–29**).

SAINT SIGHTINGS

Can you spot the saint? Use the clues below to identify each of these saints.

This saint spurs Texans to cheer: _____

This saint is an island of refuge for mariners: _____

This saint is known for her angry eruptions: _____

This saint is a sunny padre with a big naval base: _____

This saint is famous for inspiring love notes: _____

This saint is a capital guy with a better-known twin: _____

This saint gets the blame when California quakes: _____

This saint is famous for his bridge and cable cars: _____

This saint is known for his arch and cardinal virtues: _____

This saint is credited with leaving gifts under trees: _____

This saint has an Erie way of leading ships to the ocean: _____

This saint is celebrated for bringing Good News to the Irish: _____

Reproducible Page 4
Heaven or Hell: A Future Residence Guide © 2006 Concordia Publishing House. Okay to copy.

A Population Profile of Heaven & Hell

47

Home to Angels and the Saints

It has been suggested that there are three surprises in heaven:

1) the people you expected to see who are not there

2) the people you did not expect to see who are there

3) the people there who did not expect to see you

In fact, popular misunderstandings about heaven mean that many who relocate there may be pleasantly surprised by its population, which is comprised of two groups: the angels and the saints.

Angels

The angels are spirits without physical bodies who were created along with the universe to serve God. Those new to heaven are often awestruck by their majesty (**Revelation 19:9–10; 22:8–9**)! The words translated "angel" can also mean "messenger," and that is one of their chief functions: to bring messages from God to earth. Best known among angel messengers is Gabriel, who announced the rise and fall of kingdoms to the prophet Daniel (**Daniel 8:15–16; 9:20–22**), the birth of John the Baptist to the priest Zechariah (**Luke 1:11–13, 19**), and, most famously, the birth of Christ to the Virgin Mary (**Luke 1:26–27, 31**). From these events, we know that angels have names and personalities, the power to appear in human form and disappear at will, and the ability to present miraculous signs along with their messages. They are also sent to strengthen and guide people and can appear in dreams as well as in the conscious world (**Genesis 31:11; Matthew 1:20; 2:13, 19**).

Far from the chubby babies and women with wings found in many paintings, angels are often terrifying to humans who first encounter them. Daniel describes falling on his face before Gabriel, who looked like "a man dressed in linen, with a belt of the finest gold around his waist" and having a body like the gemstone chrysolite, "his face like lightning, his eyes like flaming torches, his arms and legs like the gleam of burnished bronze, and his voice like the sound of a multitude" (**Daniel 10:5–11**). In addition to serving as God's messengers, angels are also warriors and guardians, defending and protecting God's people from demons and human foes. The only angel other than Gabriel named in Scripture is Michael, who is described as "the great prince who protects your people" (**Daniel 10:13; 12:1**), an archangel sent by God to dispute with the devil (**Jude 9**), and the leader of the angel army that cast Satan and the demons out of heaven (**Revelation 12:7–9**).

Scripture tells us that there is an uncountable multitude of angels in heaven, more than "ten thousand times ten thousand" (**Daniel 7:10; Luke 2:13; Hebrews 12:22**). There are also different types or classes of angels, including cherubim (**Genesis 3:24; Psalm 80:1**), the six-winged seraphim (**Isaiah 6:2**), and archangels (**1 Thessalonians 4:16**). They do not marry or reproduce, nor can they die (**Matthew 22:30; Luke 20:35–36**). Unlike God, they do not know all mysteries, the future, or the thoughts of our hearts (**1 Kings 8:39; Matthew 24:36; 1 Peter 1:12**). However, the angels of heaven have have their hearts set on the will of God and are perfectly happy serving Him, having never sinned (**1 Timothy 5:21; Hebrews 2:16; 2 Peter 2:4**). They celebrated Christ's coming to redeem our world (**Luke 2:13**), rejoice when anyone returns to God (**Luke 15:10**), and continually praise God before His throne (**Psalm 103:20; Revelation 5:11–12; 7:11–12**).

Saints

The saints are any of God's people who have kept their faith in God and His promised salvation but are made perfect by God in heaven (**Matthew 8:11–12**). In the Bible, the words translated "saints" do not usually mean dead people or those officially recognized for miracles but all those who remain faithful in Christ, whether living or dead, who will inherit the kingdom of God prepared for them. They are described as "a great multitude that no one could count, from every nation, tribe, people and language, standing before the throne and in front of the Lamb" (**Revelation 7:9**). They are loved by God and given fine, clean linen to wear in heaven, representing their righteous acts (**Revelation 19:8**). Yet it is not their actions that makes them saints but the righteousness of Christ in which they trust (**Isaiah 64:6; Romans 4:18–25**). Therefore, they live forever in unimaginable joy, praising God with the angels and reigning with Christ over all creation (**Daniel 7:27; 1 Corinthians 6:2; Colossians 1:12; Revelation 5: 7; 14; 20; 22**).

Hell: Home to Demons and the Damned

Almost as misunderstood as the population of heaven, the residents of hell are surprisingly different from popular stereotypes. They include two groups: demons and the damned.

Demons

The demons are former angels who sinned by rebelling against God some time before mankind fell into sin. Like the good angels, they do not have physical bodies (**Ephesians 6:12**) yet still are powerful, able to possess and torment those not protected by the Holy Spirit of God (**Matthew 12:43–45; Revelation 9:2–5**). Sometimes they are allowed by God to test even his own people (**Job 1; Luke 13:11, 16**).

What Is There to Do?

Employment in Heaven and Hell

Many will come from the east and the west, and will take their places at the feast. (Matthew 8:11)

LESSON

5

Lesson Objectives

Through their study, students will begin to appreciate the blessings of heaven as well as the curses of hell.

Lesson Outline

Activity	Suggested Time	Materials Needed
Introduction and Invitation TRY THIS: *HAPPY HOLIDAYS*	10 minutes	None None
Heaven: Extreme Celebration and Recreation TRY THIS: *IMAGE IMPROVED*	20 minutes	Copies of Student Leaflet 5 Markers/colored pencils
Hell: Extreme Suffering and Destruction TRY THIS: *DEBATABLE DOUBTS*	20 minutes	Copies of Student Leaflet 5 Newsprint or white board
Conclusion and Challenge	5 minutes	None

Introduction and Invitation (10 minutes)

As your group gathers, remind them of the letters "discovered" at the last session from Screwtape, the experienced demon, to his nephew, Wormwood, on how to tempt Christians. Ask if anyone brought a Screwtape letter they had since "discovered" to share with the class. Explain that no one knows if demons write such letters, but Scripture does reveal a few things about the activities of humans in heaven and hell. The following joke or an appropriate cartoon might also be used to begin this session:

> Two ninety-year-old men, Ed and Hank, had been friends all their lives. As Ed lay dying of an illness, Hank came to visit him every day. "Ed," said Hank, "You know how we both love baseball and all the great times we had playing together, from our sandlot days through the minor leagues, and even after our retirements? I wonder if you could do me a favor. I know your faith and have no doubt you are going to be in heaven soon. When you get there, could you let me know if there's baseball in heaven?"
>
> Ed looked up from his deathbed and said, "Hank, you've always been my best friend. If it is at all possible, I'll do it for you." Shortly after that, Ed passed on.
>
> The next night, Hank had a vivid dream in which a voice called out, "Hank, Hank!"

"Who is it?" Hank heard himself respond.

"Hank, it's me, Ed."

"Ed? But you died! Where are you?"

"I'm in heaven," said Ed, "and I've got really good news and a little bad news."

"So, tell me the good news first!" said Hank.

"The good news," Ed replied, "is that there is baseball in heaven. Better yet, a lot of our old buddies are here. Better yet, we're all young men again. Better yet, it's always springtime and it never rains or snows. Better yet, we can play all we want and never get tired. Best of all, God loves baseball!"

"Really?" said Hank. "That is fantastic, beyond my wildest dreams! But what's the bad news?"

"You're pitching next Tuesday!"

Say an opening prayer.

Lord God, You have prepared a perfect place for us, beyond our wildest dreams. Guide us through Your Spirit as we study Your Word, so that we may better understand the reality that awaits us in heaven and the urgency of avoiding hell. Through Jesus, our Savior. Amen.

> **TRY THIS:** *HAPPY HOLIDAYS*
>
> Invite students to find a partner. Give pairs a minute each to describe the following to their partner: What was the happiest holiday you ever spent? Where did you go? What did you do? Who were you with? After two minutes of partner sharing, invite volunteers to share their happiest holidays with the class. Ask, **How was your experience similar to your expectation of what heaven might be like? How was it different?**

Heaven: Extreme Celebration and Recreation (20 minutes)

Hand out copies of Student Leaflet 5. Ask a student volunteer to begin reading aloud the Heaven: Extreme Celebration and Recreation section. At the end of the first paragraph, invite another student to continue the reading until the section is complete. Discuss,

What surprised you about the activities in heaven? (Answers will vary.)

How does the description differ from the way heaven is often portrayed in the media? (The media often portrays heaven as a vast empty landscape with lots of fluffy clouds, as if you were on top of the clouds in the sky. In reality, Scripture portrays heaven as a city with streets, trees, rivers, and buildings.)

What questions do you still have? (Student answers will vary. Accept all reasonable responses.)

> **TRY THIS:** *IMAGE IMPROVED*
>
> Ask your group to imagine that they are part of an agency hired to design magazine ads for heaven. Direct the students to the box titled Image Improved on the back of the Student Leaflet. Encourage them to work alone or in pairs to develop in the space an ad for heaven by drawing or writing a word picture describing what they find most appealing about heaven. Distribute colored pencils or markers, as well as other art media. Give the students seven minutes to develop their ads; then ask for volunteers to share their work with the class. Affirm their efforts!

Hell: Extreme Suffering and Destruction (20 minutes)

Direct attention to the section of the Student Leaflet titled Hell: Extreme Suffering and Destruction, and ask a volunteer to read it aloud. Discuss the following as a group:

How does the description of hell's suffering make you feel? (Some students may express feeling depressed or sad. Affirm appropriate reactions to this description.)

Did anything in the description surprise you? (Answers will vary.)

Does it affect how you feel when you hear people joke or boast about going to hell? (After reading this section, students may realize for the first time the serious nature of the suffering in hell. Help lead students to understand that hell is literally no joking matter.)

> **TRY THIS:** *DEBATABLE DOUBTS*
>
> Share the following with your group. Suppose a couple of your friends are discussing heaven and hell, when one of them makes the following statement: "I don't think I want to go to heaven. It sounds more boring than hell! Everything that's fun in this life seems to be some kind of sin, so if there is no sin in heaven, what fun will it be?" Ask your group to form at least two teams and compete to see which team can come up with the most convincing answer arguing for heaven. After forming the teams, read the statement again; then give the teams five minutes to outline their arguments and choose a representative to present their answer. On newsprint or a whiteboard, list each argument a team makes, and award one to three points, depending on how substantial the argument is. Add the points up if you want to determine the winner, but be sure to congratulate each team on its efforts.

Conclusion and Challenge (5 minutes)

Remind your group that God wants all people to be saved and sent His Son to the cross in order to experience the torments of hell so that no one else would have to. Encourage students to listen this week for comments and conversations regarding heaven and hell, praying for opportunities to confront their friends with more accurate pictures of the blessings and curses they represent.

Be sure to end with a closing prayer.

> Heavenly Father, we live in a world that often fails to take seriously what You have revealed about heaven and hell. Empower us through Your Spirit this week to share with others the urgent message of Your salvation that they may be persuaded to abandon their delusions about hell and accept the gift of heaven You have given. Through our Savior, Jesus. Amen.

Hell: Extreme Suffering and Destruction

Hell is the place to get away from it all: God, people, comfort, beauty, goodness, sound, even light itself (1 Samuel 2:9–10; 2 Thessalonians 1:9). Due to the continuous darkness, there is very little to do, apart from weeping and gnashing your teeth (Matthew 8:12; 22:13; 25:30; 2 Peter 2:17; Jude 13). The darkness is remarkable, especially given the agonizingly painful fire and burning sulfur for which hell is known (Deuteronomy 32:22; Matthew 3:12; 5:21–22; 18:8–9; Mark 9:43–48; Hebrews 10:26–27; James 3:6; Revelation 14:9–10; 20:13–15; 21:8). The only sights are those designed to increase the torment, regret, and despair, such as the sight of the saints and angels enjoying God's justice and the healing of heaven (Luke 16:23–26). There is nothing to eat or drink apart from God's wrath (Revelation 14:9–10). There is also no rest, due to the continuous nature of the torment (Revelation 14:11). Any physical body in hell is corrupted, subject to absolute agony and continual destruction (Job 26:5–6; Matthew 5:29–30; Mark 9:43–48).

> The darkness is remarkable, especially given the agonizingly painful fire and burning sulfur for which hell is known

EMPLOYMENT IN HEAVEN AND HELL

Student Leaflet 5
Heaven or Hell: A Future Residence Guide © 2006 Concordia Publishing House. Okay to copy.

Heaven: Celebration and Recreation

If you are looking for perfect fellowship with God, a place to gather with friends, healing for body and soul, an eternal feast, an escape from evil, and infinite opportunities for celebration and recreation, heaven is the place to be! Far beyond the fleeting pleasures of any "magic kingdom" on earth, God's majestic kingdom of heaven offers joy beyond imagination.

Scripture reveals that in heaven you can laugh with the Lord at the empty threats of earth (**Psalm 2:4**), even enjoying a serene safari among animals deadly in our world but harmless in His (**Isaiah 11:6–10**). The central event in heaven is the wondrous worship and perfect praise of God Himself, a celebration in which all creation shares (**Nehemiah 9:6; Revelation 5:6–13; 7:9–17; 15:2–4**). As part of the worship you are invited to the wedding supper of Christ (**Matthew 26:29; Mark 14:25; Revelation 19:9**), a chance to feast with His most famous followers (**Matthew 8:11–12**). There you can expect to receive rewards for faithful suffering and service (**Hebrews 8:5–6**) where we will behold breathtaking beauty and variety (**Revelation 21:10–14**). As God's children, we will inherit immortality (**1 Peter 1:3–5**) and reign as royalty (**Revelation 5:9–10; 22:3–5**) in a garden city where we live together with God (**Revelation 21:1–3**).

18:22–25). Though we do not know what these rewards are like, we know that they are good gifts from our giving God (**Matthew 7:9–11**). We will respond by joining all heaven in rejoicing over all those who repent and return to God (**Luke 15:7**).

There are no outsiders or strangers in heaven. You will know others and be perfectly known (**1 Corinthians 13:12**) even though your body will be resurrected imperishable, a perfected version of your earthly physique, (**1 Corinthians 15:40–43; Philippians 3:21**) similar to the resurrected body of Christ (**1 John 3:2**). You will have your own place in heaven and a sense of belonging beyond anything on earth (**2 Corinthians 5:1; Philippians 3:20; Revelation 3:12**). Every day will be a holiday, devoted to rest and recreation, and nothing you do will be like work (**Hebrews 4:9–10; Revelation 14:13**).

> There are no outsiders or strangers in heaven.

Heaven is filled with music and sound, as multitudes sing in praise of God's perfection and shout for joy (**Revelation 19:5–6**). At the same time, heaven is a place of perfect peace, with no sorrow or pain (**Revelation 21:4–5**). There is no darkness, danger, evil or impurity in heaven, but all its residents walk in the endless light of God's glory (**Revelation 21:21–27**). The Holy Spirit flows as a river through the center of the city, providing healing and perpetual fruit from the tree of life (**Revelation 22:1–2**). Therefore, nothing good is missing from heaven, and nothing bad is present.

In contrast to bland, fluffy, white, insubstantial human images of heaven, Scripture reveals a

Preparing for Your Move

Store up for yourselves treasures in heaven, where moth and rust do not destroy. (Matthew 6:20)

LESSON 6

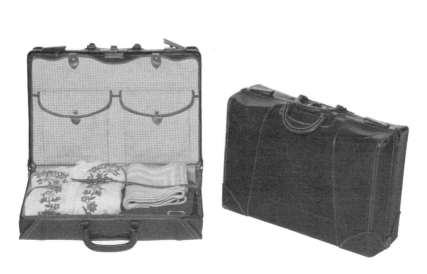

Lesson Objective

Through the study of God's Word, participants will begin to understand how our eternal destination affects our lives on earth.

Lesson Outline

Activity	Suggested Time	Materials Needed
Introduction and Invitation **TRY THIS:** *CONFIDENT CONCLUSIONS*	15 minutes	None Copies of Student Leaflet 6, envelopes from Session 1
Determine Your Destination **TRY THIS:** *PASSWORD PROMPTS*	20 minutes	Copies of Student Leaflet 6 Copies of Reproducible Page 6a
Prioritize Your Packing **TRY THIS:** *TREASURE TROVE*	15 minutes	Copies of Student Leaflet 6 Copies of Reproducible Page 6b, prizes
Conclusion and Challenge	10 minutes	None

A Note to the Leader

Please approach this lesson carefully. Some students may confuse the references to reward in heaven. Help students understand that we can do *nothing* to earn our salvation. We are saved *only* through the death and resurrection of Jesus Christ. On our own, our good works are but filthy rags. But through Christ, our good works benefit others and also the believer.

Luther says in his explanation of the Sermon on the Mount,

> Now, none of this implies any merit on our part for earning grace or Baptism or Christ and heaven, which is what they mean when they talk about merit; but it all refers to the fruit of Christianity. As we have seen, Christ is saying nothing in this sermon about how we become Christians, but only about the works and fruit that no one can do unless he already is a Christian and in a state of grace. This is evident from the words that they have to endure poverty, suffering, and persecution simply because they are Christians and have the kingdom of heaven. Now, if we are discussing the fruit that follows grace and the forgiveness of sins, we will let the terms "merit" and "reward" be used. What we oppose is the idea that works of ours like

these are the highest good, which must precede them and without which they do not take place or please God. If the insistence on grace alone without any merit is preserved, then we have no objection to giving the name "merits" to the fruit that follows. Only such statements should not be distorted and applied in an antiscriptural way to our meriting grace, but interpreted correctly, the way they were intended, as a consolation to Christians—especially when they have to suffer opposition, when they get the feeling and the impression that our life, suffering, and activity are pointless and useless. This is the consolation that Scripture uses everywhere in urging perseverance in good works. So in Jeremiah 31:16 it says: "Your works shall be rewarded"; and St. Paul says in 1 Corinthians 15:58: "In the Lord your labor is not in vain." If we did not have this consolation, we could not stand the misery, persecution, and trouble we get in exchange for doing so much good, nor let our teaching and preaching be rewarded with nothing but ingratitude and abuse. Finally we would have to stop working and suffering, though it is our obvious duty to do so.

God wants to wake us up and to strengthen us with this beautiful promise. Then we will not pay attention to the ingratitude, hate, envy, and contempt of the world, but pay attention to Him who says: "I am your God. If the world refuses to thank you and deprives you of your reputation and property, even of your body and life, just cling to Me, and find your consolation in the fact that I still have a heaven with so much in it that I can easily recompense you and give you ten times as much as they can take away from you now." And we can defy the world this way: "If it refuses to be kind to us, then it can leave, and take its kindness and everything else along. I did not start anything for its sake, and I will not do anything or stop anything for its sake. But I will do everything and suffer everything for the sake of Him whose promises are so generous and who says: 'Through Christ you already have all the treasure in heaven, and more than enough. Yet I will give you even more, as a bonus. You will have the kingdom of heaven revealed to you, and the Christ whom you now have in faith you will have in sight as well, in eternal glory and joy, the more you suffer and labor now.' " (AE 21:291)

Introduction and Invitation (15 minutes)

As your group gathers, ask whether they encountered any comments or conversations regarding heaven and hell this past week and how they responded. Explain to the class that this session will consider how we can have confidence that heaven is our final destination and that we even store up treasure there. The following joke or an appropriate cartoon might also be used to begin this session:

A famous politician dies suddenly and finds himself at the gates of heaven. There a crowd gathers around the man and an angel greets him, "Welcome to heaven! We are all excited to see you—and very curious. I have instructions for you unlike any I've seen before. It seems that your life on earth made your personal beliefs unclear, so you are going to be allowed to tour both heaven and hell for three days each and then make a choice between the two."

The politician was quite pleased at this special privilege and greatly enjoyed his tour of heaven. He observed the awesome spectacle of ongoing worship before God's throne, the perfect paradise of the New Jerusalem, and the blissful wedding feast of the Lamb.

In what seemed like no time at all, he was solemnly escorted to a special elevator, where he descended all day down to hell. There he was quite surprised to find what appeared to be a pleasant country club where everyone seemed young and attractive, enjoying endless games of golf, buffets of lobster and caviar, free drinks, and designer drugs. Satan also seemed far different than expected: telling jokes and mingling, he was the life of the party. Best of all, most of the man's old friends were there, remembering old times and encouraging him to join them.

When the three days were finally over, the politician was escorted back to the elevator for the long trip back to heaven, where he was again met by the angel at the gate. "Well," the angel asked, "having seen both heaven and hell, it is time for you to decide: where would you like to spend eternity?"

The man replied, "You know, on earth I never would have dreamed it would be such a close call. Heaven is beautiful, and I have a great deal of respect for God, but I have to say, I think I would be more comfortable spending eternity in hell."

"So be it," said the angel. "You've made your decision."

At that, the man was escorted back to the elevator and returned to hell. When he arrived, the politician was stunned to find that hell looked like it had been hit by a bomb. The beautiful club was now a dark, filthy, fetid, painfully hot dungeon. His mouth instantly dried and his skin began to blister. None of his friends could be seen, but distant screams of agony could be heard. With relief, the man noticed Satan coming to meet him, still smiling and seemingly unchanged.

"What happened?" The politician asked. "Just yesterday the place was totally different!"

"My friend," Satan replied, "Yesterday we were campaigning; today you voted!"

Say an opening prayer.

Lord God, You have revealed the glories of heaven awaiting all who trust in You, as well as the horrors of hell awaiting all who reject You. Give us wisdom as we study Your Word today so that we might not only avoid the deceptions of Your enemy, but also lead others to trust in You and receive the reward You have prepared. Through Christ Jesus. Amen.

TRY THIS: *CONFIDENT CONCLUSIONS*

Hand out copies of Student Leaflet 6, along with the envelopes students completed during the Confidential Conclusions exercise in Session 1. If some students were not present at Session 1, do not give them other students' envelopes; simply inform them that the survey questions under Confident Conclusions are the same. Instruct all students to use the Session 6 version to retake the survey, looking up the Bible verses that follow questions for any they are unsure about. When students are finished, invite them to open their envelopes and compare their earlier answers with their current conclusions to see if any of their answers have changed. As a group, discuss each question and any Scripture verses or learning from a previous session that might help answer the question.

1. **Only old people really need to think about death. Ecclesiastes 11:8–9** (No. Young people do not know when they will die and ought to keep death and God's judgment in mind.)

2. **Children who die are considered innocent before God. Psalm 51:5** (No. Children are considered sinful from birth and in need of God's forgiveness.)

3. **A few people, like Hitler, are bad, but most are basically good. Romans 3:21–24** (No. All people are sinful in the eyes of God and will be judged by Him.)

4. **God sends good people to heaven and only really bad people to hell. Matthew 21:23–32** (No. God welcomes to heaven bad people who repent and rejects good people who reject Him.)

5. **God created hell as a place to punish people who make Him angry. Matthew 25:41** (No. God created hell to confine and punish the angels who had rebelled against Him.)

6. **Heaven is a quiet, airy place where spirits float around on clouds. Revelation 19:1–6** (No. Heaven is a substantial place of loud celebration where believers enjoy perfected human bodies.)

7. **Hell is an interesting place where you can party with famous people. 2 Peter 2:4–9** (No. Hell is a gloomy place of torment and solitary confinement.)

8. **Heaven is whatever you want it to be, which is different for everyone. Revelation 21:3–4** (No. Heaven is the dwelling place of God with His people—perfect for us, but not dependent on us.)

9. **After you die, your spirit comes back as a different person or animal. Hebrews 9:27–28** (No. After you die, you are personally resurrected once to face God's judgment and eternal life or death.)

10. **When small children or really good people die they become angels. Luke 20:35–36** (No. Humans in heaven will be unmarried and immortal like angels, but humans do not become angels.)

11. **Spirits of those who die tragically can hang around and haunt places. Luke 11:24–26** (No. Human spirits await judgment in heaven or hell, and demons seem to rest in people, not places.)

12. **There are no guarantees regarding where you go when you die. Ephesians 1:13–14** (No. Scripture makes it clear that believers are guaranteed heaven and unbelievers are guaranteed hell.)

Determine Your Destination (20 minutes)

Direct your group's attention to the section of the Student Leaflet titled Determine Your Destination, and invite a volunteer to read it aloud. Switch to different volunteers to read The Gateway to God and The Highway to Hell. Discuss,

How do the paths to God and away from God differ? (The way to heaven is through faith in Christ; the road to hell is through lack of faith in Christ. The road to hell is broad, because many factors can lead to a rejection of Christ; the gate to heaven is narrow, because only God's Spirit can produce saving faith in Christ. The road to heaven was built by God; the road to hell is of human origin. The road to hell often produces selfish and destructive behaviors; the gate to heaven is usually reflected in godly and creative behaviors. Other answers are possible.)

Are there any ways in which the paths are similar? (Both are revealed by Scripture, both have to do with the conditions of our hearts, and both can be guaranteed!)

> **TRY THIS: *PASSWORD PROMPTS***
>
> One simple visual illustration of the way to heaven is often referred to as "The Bridge." A person wishing to share Christ with another might first sketch a chasm, labeling the bank on the left "man" and the bank on the right "God," then describing what Scripture tells us: "All have sinned and fall short of the glory of God" (Romans 3:23). Arrows drawn from "man" into the chasm represent the futility of all human efforts to reach God due to our sin. Then a bridge in the shape of a cross is drawn from "God" to "man," representing God's gift of Christ Jesus, who became human and died to reconcile us with God and create a pathway for us to God through His sacrifice.
>
> Distribute copies of Reproducible Page 6a. Share "The Bridge" illustration

with your group, then invite them to come up with their own Password Prompt: a simple illustration of the gift given by Christ who has opened the way for us to God when all human efforts fail. In order to help students get started, encourage them to read the "I Am" statements concerning Jesus from the Gospel of John, printed on the Reproducible Page.

"I am the living bread that came down from heaven. If anyone eats of this bread, he will live forever. This bread is My flesh, which I will give for the life of the world" (John 6:51).

"I am the light of the world. Whoever follows Me will never walk in darkness, but will have the light of life" (John 8:12).

"I am the gate; whoever enters through Me will be saved. He will come in and go out, and find pasture" (John 10:9).

"I am the good shepherd. The good shepherd lays down His life for the sheep" (John 10:11).

"I am the resurrection and the life. He who believes in Me will live, even though he dies; and whoever lives and believes in Me will never die" (John 11:25–26).

"I am the way and the truth and the life. No one comes to the Father except through Me" (John 14:6).

"I am the vine; you are the branches. If a man remains in Me and I in him, he will bear much fruit; apart from Me you can do nothing. If anyone does not remain in Me, he is like a branch that is thrown away and withers; such branches are picked up, thrown into the fire and burned" (John 15:5–6).

Prioritize Your Packing (15 minutes)

Direct your group's attention to the Student Leaflet section titled Prioritize Your Packing, and invite volunteers to read this section. Discuss the following together:

In what sense is it true when they say, "You can't take it with you"? (We cannot take any physical thing with us to our eternal destination.)

In what sense is it untrue—what can we take with us? (We can take with us our personal identities as God's people or God's enemies and the record of our obedience and disobedience for judgment and punishment or reward.)

TRY THIS: *TREASURE TROVE*

Invite students to pair up for a Bible Treasure Hunt, and challenge them to look up the verses on the Student Leaflet and write down what behaviors earn "treasure in heaven." Consider rewarding each team when they complete their search, perhaps with coin-shaped chocolates, a "$10,000 Bar," or other appropriate prize. Make sure you have enough for each team to be rewarded.

Matthew 5:11–12 "Blessed are you when people insult you . . . because of Me. . . . Great is your reward."

Matthew 5:19 "Whoever practices and teaches these commands will be called great in the kingdom of heaven."

Matthew 6:1–2 "Give to the needy, do not announce it. . . . They have received their reward in full."

Matthew 6:16–18 "When you fast . . . your Father, who sees what is done in secret, will reward you."

Matthew 10:41–42 "Anyone who receives a prophet because he is a prophet will receive a prophet's reward."

Matthew 18:4 "Whoever humbles himself like this child is the greatest in the kingdom of heaven."

Matthew 19:16–21 "Sell your possessions and give to the poor, and you will have treasure in heaven."

Matthew 19:29 "Everyone who has left houses . . . for my sake will receive a hundred times as much."

Luke 6:35–36 "But love your enemies, do good to them, and lend to them. . . . Your reward will be great."

Ephesians 6:7–8 "Serve wholeheartedly . . . because you know that the Lord will reward everyone for whatever good he does."

Hebrews 11:25–26 "He regarded disgrace for the sake of Christ as of greater value . . . because he was looking ahead to his reward."

Revelation 2:10 "Be faithful, even to the point of death, and I will give you the crown of life."

Conclusion and Challenge (10 minutes)

Encourage your group to continue considering this life as preparation for eternal life, confident of God's guaranteed grace given through Christ, and packing their days with Christlike conduct. To reinforce this final point, share a fitting cartoon, or tell the following joke:

> A very wealthy woman came to faith late in life and immediately began redirecting her riches to support the work of the Church and various charities. Upon her death, she was taken to heaven, where she delighted in the presence of God and reunited with many old friends. One day as she walked through paradise, she was overjoyed to meet the person who had introduced her to the Lord, her former chauffeur, out for a drive in a shiny red sports car. After a long and happy conversation, she asked him about the car.

"Oh," he said, "it's part of my heavenly reward. You are welcome to drive it if you like, or you could go to the Claims Department to see what they have reserved for you."

She thanked him for the offer but resolved to seek out the Claims Department, curious as to what she might be given. Directed by her friend, she soon found the front desk of what looked like a giant auto dealership. There she gave her name to an angel and was escorted to one of many huge warehouses, where she was given her choice from among thousands of shiny new bicycles.

"I don't understand," she wondered. "My former chauffeur is driving a sports car. Why do I get a bicycle?"

"Its part of the reward system in heaven," the angel answered. "The extent to which you shared your faith, time, talents, and wealth on earth to promote God's kingdom compared to how much you were given must have been somewhat less than your friend."

Immediately recognizing the perfect justice of this arrangement, the woman nodded, smiled, and chose one of the bicycles, which fit her perfectly. The angel watched her ride away happily, but as the woman left the dealership she became distracted, veered off the bike path, and crashed into some shrubs. Concerned, the angel rushed over to find her sprawled in the grass, laughing hysterically.

"What happened?" the angel asked.

"Oh," she gasped, "I just saw my former pastor go by on roller skates!"

Be sure to end with a closing prayer.

Heavenly Father, thank You for not treating us as our sins deserve but for sending Your Son as our gate into Your presence, now and forever. Empower us through Your Spirit to share Your salvation through the ways we live our lives that we may store up treasure in heaven and invite others to join us there. Through Jesus, our Lord and Savior. Amen.

Any route other than trusting God for salvation through Jesus Christ, no matter how popular or scenic or well paved with good intentions, eventually leads to hell. That's why Jesus said, "Wide is the gate and broad is the road that leads to destruction, and many enter through it" (**Matthew 7:13**). Some travelers openly embrace this road in defiance of God and His Word (**Philippians 3:18–19**), while many others are merely deceived about their destination or ignorant regarding the condemnation that results from rejecting Christ in their hearts (**Matthew 10:33; Mark 16:16; John 3:18, 36; 2 Thessalonians 1:8–10; Revelation 20:12–15**).

Prioritize Your Packing

Even though God Himself has prepared a place for you in heaven and already paid for your entry through Christ, you are strongly encouraged to make a priority of packing your life in preparation for your move and storing up treasure in heaven. Jesus urged His followers, "Do not store up for yourselves treasures on earth, where moth and rust destroy, and where thieves break in and steal. But store up for yourselves treasures in heaven, where moth and rust do not destroy, and where thieves do not break in and steal. For where your treasure is, there your heart will be also" (**Matthew 6:19–21**). To be a citizen of heaven in this world is, after all, to be an ambassador of God in a foreign land, working to do His will and represent Him (**2 Corinthians 5:19–20**). Therefore, on Judgment Day, Jesus will not only look in the book of life to see if you have reserved a place in heaven by faith, but He will also look through the book of your works to see what reward you have earned in heaven (**Matthew 16:27; Revelation 20:12–15; 22:12**).

We do not know exactly what the rewards will be like, but the term treasures implies that they are valuable and glorious. We do not know what kind of works earn them, because Scripture is full of God's guidance on how we ought to live and work. Paul also gives this important packing tip: since they will be subject to the fire of God's judgment in transit, our works ought to be of genuine quality and based on what Christ has done for us (**1 Corinthians 3:11–15**).

It is also possible to pack your life full of works and priorities that store up God's wrath for you in hell (**Romans 2:5–8**). Just as Scripture implies various amounts of glory for God's saints in heaven, it alludes to various amounts of condemnation on Judgment Day for those on their way to hell (**Matthew 10:14–15; 11:20–24; 23:15**). The most severe punishment is for those who were given much and knew what God expected but failed to take Him seriously (**Matthew 7:21–23; Luke 12:47–48**).

Heaven or Hell: A Future Residence Guide © 2006 Concordia Publishing House. Okay to copy.

After each statement from the first session of this study, circle "**yes**" or "**no**." If you are still a bit unsure, look up the Bible verse that follows. Compare your conclusions with responses you may have written in the first session, and prepare to discuss them with the group.

1. Only old people really need to think about death.

   Yes   No

   Ecclesiastes 11:8–9

2. Children who die are considered innocent before God.

   Yes   No

   Psalm 51:5

3. A few people, like Hitler, are bad, but most are basically good.

   Yes   No

   Romans 3:21–24

4. God sends good people to heaven and only really bad people to hell.

   Yes   No

   Matthew 21:23–32

5. God created hell as a place to punish people who make Him angry.

   Yes   No

   Matthew 25:41

6. Heaven is a quiet, airy place where spirits float around on clouds.

   Yes   No

   Revelation 19:1–6

7. Hell is an interesting place where you can party with famous people.

   Yes   No

   2 Peter 2:4–9

8. Heaven is whatever you want it to be, which is different for everyone.

   Yes   No

   Revelation 21:3–4

9. After you die, your spirit comes back as a different person or animal.

   Yes   No

   Hebrews 9:27–28

10. When small children or really good people die they become angels.

    Yes   No

    Luke 20:35–36

11. Spirits of those who die tragically can hang around and haunt places.

    Yes   No

    Luke 11:24–26

12. There are no guarantees regarding where you go when you die.

    Yes   No

    Ephesians 1:13–14

Determine Your Destination

Now that you have had a chance to tour heaven and hell, learned a little about their histories and populations, and considered their respective employment opportunities, you probably have a strong preference regarding which place you would like to be your future residence. The question may well have arisen, "How do I know which place will be my destination?" Determining the location of your future residence is comp... you believe.

The Gateway to God

In order to remain a community that is completely exclusive of all evil, sin, sorrow, pain, death, and anything outside the will of God, Scripture reveals that heaven is a gated community with only one gate **(John 14:1–6)**. However, anyone willing to leave evil and become a child of God through faith is welcome to enter through that gate, which is Jesus Christ Himself **(John 10:9; Revelation 21:27; 22:14)**! Therefore, "whoever believes in Him shall not perish but have eternal life" **(John 3:16, 18, 36; 6:40; 17:1–3; Matthew 10:32)**. Contrary to popular jokes and misconceptions that entry into heaven is based on good works, ability to pass a test, or anything we do for God, Scripture reveals that entry into heaven is a free gift that comes through faith in what God has done for us through the death and resurrection of Jesus **(Romans 3:20–24; 5:1–2; Galatians 3:22; Ephesians 2:4–9; 3:12; Philippians 3:8–9; 2 Thessalonians 1:8–10)**. If God has brought you to trust in His Son, Jesus, who died in your place and rose to bring you forgiveness, you are already a child of God, born again into His family, and a citizen of heaven with a place reserved for you there **(John 1:12–13; 5:24; 10:28; Galatians 3:26–27)**.

This offer is made available to all people, regardless of their age, gender, or race, through Baptism and God's Word **(Matthew 18:1–4; Mark 16:15–16; Galatians 3:26–28; 2 Timothy 3:14–15)**. However, it is a limited-time offer, good only during your lifetime **(Luke 13:24–30)**! God desires that all people be saved; therefore, Jesus urged, "Enter through the narrow gate. For wide is the gate and broad is the road that leads to destruction, and many enter through it. But small is the gate and narrow the road that leads to life, and only a few find it" **(Matthew 7:13–14)**.

Password Prompts

"I am the living bread that came down from heaven. If anyone eats of this bread, he will live forever. This bread is My flesh, which I will give for the life of the world" (**John 6:51**).

"I am the light of the world. Whoever follows Me will never walk in darkness, but will have the light of life" (**John 8:12**).

"I am the gate; whoever enters through Me will be saved. He will come in and go out, and find pasture" (**John 10:9**).

"I am the good shepherd. The good shepherd lays down His life for the sheep" (**John 10:11**).

"I am the resurrection and the life. He who believes in Me will live, even though he dies; and whoever lives and believes in Me will never die" (**John 11:25–26**).

"I am the way and the truth and the life. No one comes to the Father except through Me" (**John 14:6**).

"I am the vine; you are the branches. If a man remains in Me and I in him, he will bear much fruit; apart from Me you can do nothing. If anyone does not remain in Me, he is like a branch that is thrown away and withers; such branches are picked up, thrown into the fire and burned" (**John 15:5–6**).

Reproducible Page 6a
Heaven or Hell: A Future Residence Guide © 2006 Concordia Publishing House. Okay to copy.

Treasure Trove

What behaviors do the following verses describe as rewarded in heaven?

Matthew 5:11–12

Matthew 5:19

Matthew 6:1–2

Matthew 6:16–18

Matthew 10:41–42

Matthew 18:4

Matthew 19:16–21

Matthew 19:29

Luke 6:35–36

Ephesians 6:7–8

Hebrews 11:25–26

Revelation 2:10

Reproducible Page 6b
Heaven or Hell: A Future Residence Guide © 2006 Concordia Publishing House. Okay to copy.